GET YOUR FINANCIAL LIFE

IN ORDER

Simple Tips on Budgeting and
Household Finance

Lisa Michaels

**Braughler™
Books**

Cover photo: ID 70011683 © Allan Swart | 123RF

Printed in the United States of America
Published by Braughler Books LLC., Springboro, Ohio
First printing, 2023
ISBN: 978-1-955791-60-1

Library of Congress Control Number: 2023907854

Ordering information: Special discounts are available on quantity purchases by bookstores, corporations, associations, and others. For details, contact the publisher at: sales@braughlerbooks.com or at 937-58-BOOKS

For questions or comments about this book, please write to: info@braughlerbooks.com

Braughler™
Books
braughlerbooks.com

CONTENTS

Introduction

Are you someone who constantly lives paycheck to paycheck? Are you always behind on your bills or can't ever
seem to get ahead? Is your financial life an unorganized
nightmare? Do you have poor credit and bad spending
habits? Well, if you are looking for easy to follow steps
that can help you get your financial life on track then
this book is for you. This is not a book about how to make
money or to get rich. It is simply about how to manage
your money and build and keep a budget that works for
you. I have included some other helpful tips on how to
save money and build credit as well. I am self-taught
but have learned a lot about money and credit over the
years through my own experiences. The purpose of this
book is to help others get on track with their financial life
and be able to build and plan for the future. I see a lot of
people who are unorganized with their bills and struggle
every day. Well, you don't have to. If you live within your
means and stay on track with your budget, you won't have
to stress about money, no matter how much or how little
you make. A wise business man (my grandpa) once told
me, it's not about what you make, it's about what you do
with it. With a little discipline and organization, you can
be on your way to a brighter financial future!

1. GETTING ORGANIZED

Being organized plays a huge part in your finances. If you have mail scattered all over the house and don't know what's what, it's going to be hard to pay your bills on time. When you bring in your mail, do not just throw it aside in a pile for later. Sort through it as soon as you bring it inside and pull out all the bills and whatever else may be important. You can set the junk mail aside for another time if you do not feel like going through all of it. Take all of your bills and put them in your designated bill area. If you do not have one, then it's time to start one. Get a folder or tray that you can put all of your bills in. If you put them in a folder, you can mark one side of the folder 'unpaid' and the other side 'paid'. Then when it's time to pay bills for the week, you can look through them and see what needs paid. Try to pay everything once a week. After you get paid, see what bills are due before your next paycheck and just pay all of them for the week on that one day. For example, on Friday, pay all of your bills that are due from that day until the next Friday. Or if you get paid every two weeks, you can pay everything that is due over the next two weeks. Do not be afraid to pay a bill early. If you have the money and something is due within a week or two, just go ahead and pay it and get it out of the way. After you pay a bill, write PAID on it and the date you paid it. Even if you schedule it to be paid a few days out, write the date that it will come out of your account. This helps to eliminate confusion and you will not have to wonder if you have paid it or not.

If you have other important papers, but you are not sure where to put them, get a folder, write your name on the front, and keep them in there. You can do this for your spouse too. You should have one for yourself and one for your spouse, and if there is something important that belongs to them, put it in their folder and they can decide what to do with it from there. Even if it's just important notes or something you wrote down that you want to keep, put it in there. These folders will be a life saver for you and your spouse if you keep up on it. If you are looking for an important paper or some notes that you have taken, you know they will be in that folder. Be sure not to put bills in that folder though. Bills should have their own designated area. These personal folders should be for other things that you want to keep in a safe place. It can be something as simple as some notes that you took from something you saw on tv or the internet that you want to reference later. Or maybe you got a letter in the mail that isn't time sensitive but you want to look at it later, you can put things like that in your folder.

After you have paid your bills, do not throw them away. Keep them in a filing cabinet or a file folder. You can make a folder in your filing cabinet for paid bills. Start new every January and have a sticky flag for each different bill. For the first bill of the year, put a sticky flag on the end of that paper so that it sticks out. As the year goes on, you will have all of your electric bills in order, gas, phone, etc. It is easy to reference later on if you need to go back and look at something. At the end of the year, you can take all of them out and rubber band them together and write the year on it and put them in storage. Some people like to keep all of their bills for at least 5 years, but it is totally up to you how long you want to keep them. You can also make a folder for your job, your house (things you buy or upgrades to the house), your car (maintenance and receipts), medical etc. If you are able to have a small filing cabinet or even a box with file folders in it, it will make your life a lot easier to have all of your bills and important papers organized. If paper filing isn't your thing, you can certainly do it electronically. Upload whichever documents you want to keep to your computer and have separate folders for them on there.

Do you ever get coupons in the mail for the grocery or restaurants? It's easy for them to get lost and tossed aside, but there is a way to keep them somewhat organized if you want to keep them. You can cut out all the grocery coupons that you think you may use and paperclip them together. You can organize them by date, having the ones that will expire the soonest on top and keep them in a kitchen drawer. Each time you go to the store you can pick out which coupons you think you will use and take them with you. The coupons you get for restaurants or home repairs, you can cut them out and clip them together on the side of your refrigerator. Then when you want to go out to eat, look through them and see if you have any coupons you would like to use. You could also put a small white board on your refrigerator or a note pad where you write down items that you need to buy. As soon as you are running low on an item or run out completely, write it on the white board or note pad. That way when you go to make your grocery list, you know exactly what you need. When you get back home from the store, cross off the items that you have bought off the white board.

A good tip for grocery shopping is to add up the cost of the items you are buying as you put them in your cart. As you pick things up that you want to buy, write down the price and add it up as you go. If you bring a paper list to the store (not one on your phone) you can add up the cost of the items on your piece of paper. If you have good basic math skills you can do this instead of using the calculator on your phone. It can be easy to push the wrong button on a calculator and lose track of where you are, especially on a touch screen phone. Nonetheless, if you keep a running total as you shop, you will not spend more than you wanted to when you get to the checkout. For example, if you know you only have $50 to spend at the store, it helps to add up the items as you put them in your cart, so you do not over-spend when you get to the checkout. Another good tip for grocery shopping is to buy all the necessities, or items on your list first. Don't pick up impulse items until you have first picked up the items that you went there for. Then if you still have more money to spend, after you have picked up your necessities, you can go back and get other things you may want that are not on your list. You can also do your grocery shopping online too and schedule a time to pick it up. This works good for people with busy schedules who may not have enough time in their day to go into the store and grocery shop.

Staying organized is such an important part of your financial life. Not everyone is good at being organized but that doesn't mean you can't give it a try. Even if you can't be as organized as you would like, having everything in one place is a good start. Keep all of your bills and important papers in one area of your home, preferably on a desk or in your home office if you have one. This will help you keep track of everything and not be searching all over your home when it is time to pay bills.

2. HOW TO MAKE A BUDGET

Do you know how much your monthly bills are all together? Weekly? Yearly? Do you know how much money you need just to survive? Don't feel bad if you don't. Lots of people don't know. They live paycheck to paycheck and they just hope and assume they will have enough money to pay a bill when it comes in. But you do not have to live this way. You can be certain of how much money you need to pay all your bills, and have some left over every month. Let's look at some ways to budget your money.

In order to make a budget you have to break everything down and look at all of your expenses. Let's look at all of your regular bills that you pay every month (or quarterly) and see if we can get a total number. Now what I like to do is to break everything down to get a weekly, monthly, and yearly total of all of your bills. This way you can budget your outgoing money and figure out how much money you need out of each paycheck to cover everything. Let's look at an example page of everything broken down.

Bills	Year
Rent/Mortgage: $1,000	$12,000
Car Payment: $350	$4,200
Car Insurance: $130	$1,560
Cell Phone: $120	$1,440
Internet: $60	$720
Electric: $80	$960
Gas: $80	$960
TV: $100	$1,200
Water/Trash: $50	$600
TOTAL	**$23,640**

$23,640 yearly total of outgoing money;
$1,970 monthly; $455 weekly

Write down all of your regular bills on the left side, then multiply them by 12 (12 months) to get the yearly total. For bills that are variable, like electric and gas; take your last 12 bills, add them together, then divide by 12 to get a monthly average. If you have bills that are quarterly, like water and trash; take your last 4 bills and add them together, then divide by 12 to get a monthly average. Once you have all of your bills written down along with the yearly totals, you can add up all the numbers in the yearly column to get a yearly total of outgoing money.

Even if you have bills that aren't going to last the whole year, include them anyway. For example, if you are paying on something and you only have 2-3 months left to pay on it, write it down anyway. It is easier to budget if you include everything and you can adjust and rewrite your sheet as your bills change.

When you lay everything out on paper and get a yearly total of your outgoing money, it's a lot easier to see what you have and to budget it. You can divide your yearly total by 12 to get a monthly total, or divide your yearly total by 52 to get a weekly total. It is better to divide the yearly total by 52 to get your weekly total than to divide the monthly total by 4 because it will not be accurate. There are 4.3 weeks in a month, not 4 so if you want an accurate weekly total you have to divide the yearly total by 52.

Depending on how you get paid; whether it is weekly or bi-weekly, you can now determine how much money you need out of each paycheck to cover all of your bills. I've found the easiest way for me to cover my bills is to keep my bill money separate from my spending money. If you are able to open a separate checking account just for bills, it is easier to manage. Most banks will let you open a second checking under the same account, so that if you use online banking, everything is on one screen and you can transfer money between the accounts. You will get a separate debit card for the new checking account so you don't get the two confused. If your debit cards look the same like mine do, since they are from the same bank, you can write with sharpie on the back of them which account they go to. You can put money into your bills account from each paycheck and you should always have enough money in there to pay your bills. If you are unable to open a second checking account, then calculate how much you need to leave in your account to pay bills, and the difference will be your spending money. You can take out your spending money in cash if you like so you don't lose track of how much you can afford to spend that week. If you budget right and get the correct weekly total for your outgoing money, you will never have to worry if you have enough money to pay your regular bills. As your bills change, update your budget sheet and adjust the money you need to take out of each paycheck. There are probably millions of ways out there to balance a budget, but this is just one example that will surely take the guesswork out of your monthly bills.

TIPS:

— **It doesn't hurt to put in an extra $10 per week to cover unexpected rises in your bills.**

— **Don't use bill money for anything other than bills.** Remember you budgeted to have enough money for everything, so if you think you have extra, it is probably needed for an upcoming bill. You will put in the same amount of money out of each check to cover your bills. For example, if you deposit $500 each time to cover your bills, and your bills for the week are only $200; leave the rest of the money in there because that money is budgeted for the whole month so it will be used for a bill the next week or the week after.

If you are someone who struggles to pay bills on time or forgets to pay them, write them down! Get a calendar and put it on the wall of the room that you pay bills in. You can write on the calendar what day each bill is due, or you can get some small post it flags and place them on your calendar. After you pay a bill, move the flag to the correct day of the next month that the bill will come due again. If you have a lot of things that are financed like cars, interest free credit card promotions, or you have bought something at a store that is interest free for a year or two, write it all down together. Get a notebook and write all of your debt on one page. Write down the total balance of each loan or credit card, when it is due, how much the payment is and when it has to be paid off to avoid interest. Each week after you pay bills, rewrite all of the same debt on a new page. Update any changes, and if the balance has gone down or up, or if the payment date has changed. Here is an example of what that sheet could look like:

Car loan: $23,756.84 (8-14)...........$350 (payoff 3-14-27)

Truck loan: $5,392.38 (8-23) ....$200 (payoff 12-23-24)

Signature loan: $3,000 (8-2)..........$100 (payoff 7-2-23)

Credit card: $376.86 (8-7)...............$50
(pay in full to avoid interest)

Furniture: $3,498.48 (8-10)............$100 (payoff 11-10-23)

Total Debt: $36,024.56 (-$123.82)

The column on the left shows the total remaining balance on the loan. Then it shows the next due date for when it has to be paid. To the right of that shows the monthly payment amount, then the maturity date of the loan. If you have something that has to be paid in full to avoid interest, write that down so you can try to pay it off completely to avoid interest.

TIP:

When you look at your credit card statement, the statement balance is what you have to pay to avoid being charged interest. The remaining balance after you pay the statement balance will be carried over to next month's billing cycle and you will not be charged interest if you pay the statement balance again the following month. **If you can afford to pay the entire balance of the card, go ahead and pay it and get it out of the way.** If you can help it, try not to get into the habit of only paying the minimum payment on your cards. This is how you can rack up interest and get into a lot of bad debt in a hurry.

At the bottom of the sheet it shows the total debt of all of the loans. In parenthesis it shows the difference from the week before. You can make a new sheet every week and compare the total difference from the week before. This is a good way to display all of your debt in one place and really see what you have. Another helpful tip is anytime you finance something with no interest, figure out how many months you have to pay the loan off and divide the total balance by the number of months to get the monthly payment. Do not pay the minimum payment because you will not pay the loan off in time. For example, if you finance something for $2,400 and they give you one year to pay on it with no interest, then you will need to pay $200 a month to pay it off in time. The more organized you are with your bills, the easier things will be. You will know exactly what you owe and when you owe it. Then you can utilize that information to be more calculated when making financial decisions in the future.

3. DEALING WITH UNEXPECTED BILLS/ EXPENSES

What do you do when you have an unexpected bill or expense? Panic! Oh my, what am I going to do?! Don't panic. It happens to everyone and it will not be the death of you. It depends on how much money you need as to what your options are. Do you need $50? $100? $200? $1,000 or more? Let's see what your options are.

Maybe you have a savings account or a family member or friend you can borrow from. These are your easiest options. But if you borrow money from someone, make a real plan to pay them back. For example, tell them you can pay them $20 a week until they are paid back and keep a record of it. The last thing you need is for your loved ones to not trust you and deny you help in the future.

If savings or borrowing money aren't an option, maybe you have a credit card you can use. Just make sure you pay it back in a timely manner so that you aren't charged a bunch of interest. And you will want the available credit back in case you need it again in the future.

You could try going to the bank and asking for a signature loan. This requires credit approval but you can ask your bank of your approval odds before you apply. If you have a vehicle that is paid off you can apply for a collateral loan. The bank holds the title to your car until you pay back the loan.

If your expense is really big and you own a house, you could see about taking an equity loan out on your house. Call your lender that owns your mortgage and see what your options are. This usually requires them to re-appraise your house, but it's not too difficult. The lender should take care of everything for you and walk you through the process. Just be aware that whatever amount you take out will be added to the current amount owed and your monthly house payment may go up.

Do you have a 401k through your employer? Most companies will let you take a loan out on your own money. Sometimes you can take a lump sum out without paying it back, but you will pay a high tax rate on it. Talk to your employer and see how they can help.

Do you own anything of value? Jewelry? Coins? Guns? Tools? Musical instruments? Take it to a pawn shop! You can sell your items and they will make you a cash offer on them, or you can pawn it. If you pawn your items, they will hold it and loan you money based on what the item is worth. You pay the loan back with interest, and when it is paid off you get your item back. This isn't the best option if you are tight for cash because the loans are normally short term and have to be paid back quickly. And it gives you another bill to pay. But if it makes sense for you, then do it. You could also try selling stuff online to get some quick cash. There are multiple sites out there for selling things or you could also try having a yard sale.

There are lots of options out there if you need money fast. You just have to decide which option is best for you. You should also make a plan in the future so that you are better prepared for the unexpected.

4. CUTTING BACK ON YOUR EXPENSES

Let's face it. We all spend money on things that we do not need. That's part of enjoying life, right? Well, if you're trying to save money, there are probably some unnecessary expenses that you can cut out. It's easy to spend all of your money for the week and not know where it went. If you find yourself in this situation, let's see how we can fix it.

If you do not know where all of your money goes, maybe it's time to start keeping track of it. Do you get coffee a lot during the week? Go through a drive-thru? Go to the vending machine a lot at work? Start keeping track of it! Get a journal and write down what you buy and how much you spend each time. You would be surprised how much a couple dollars here and there adds up.

If you find yourself buying snacks a lot while you are out, maybe you should start getting those things at the grocery store. Especially drinks too. There is a very high mark-up on those items for convenience. Try buying these things at the grocery store and throwing them in your bag to take to work, or when you are out running errands. If you are going to be out and about for most of the day, take a granola bar, or some fruit or some other snack with you in case you get hungry. This will keep you from running through a drive thru or getting snacks at the gas station. If there is something you drink a lot of, buy it in bulk at a warehouse store if you have a membership. (Usually, the price is less than $1 per can/bottle when you buy them in bulk). It's ok to treat yourself once or twice a week to go out, but if you are doing it every day then you are just wasting your money.

Stop teasing yourself. If you do not have any money to spend, then do not go shopping; even online. It can be so tempting to shop online and just 'browse' at things. But odds are you are going to find something you like and want to buy it. Stop doing this! You are not doing yourself any good by spending money that you do not have. Unless it is an absolute necessity at that time, do not buy it if you do not have the money.

Do not let your friends and family create bad habits for you. If you have friends or family that like to go out a lot and you cannot afford it, tell them. Most likely they will understand. Tell them you cannot afford a certain place, or you do not have the money that day that you will have to go another day. They may offer to pay for you, or you can reschedule. It is good to go out and have a good time but do not go into debt over it if you cannot afford it.

Are you someone who has to have name brand everything? If you can afford it, great! But most people cannot. Most people do not care where your clothes came from or who made them. And if the people you hang around do care, then maybe you need new friends! Do what makes you happy and do not worry about what others think about you. You can get very nice clothes for cheap if you shop right. When you go into a clothing store, shop the sale rack first. Or try to buy things off-season. Buy summer clothes at the end of the summer and winter clothes at the end of the winter. Usually, the stores have them marked down quite a bit because they are trying to make room for the next season. Try shopping second-hand stores too. Usually, they are all name brand and still in pretty good shape.

There are all kinds of ways to shop smart and save money. If you feel like you are spending too much money, then start keeping track of it. Re-evaluate all of your extra expenses and see where you need to make changes. Do what makes the most sense for you and do not forget to enjoy yourself along the way.

5. HOW TO BUILD/REPAIR YOUR CREDIT

Do you have bad credit or no credit? Credit is a great tool if you use it correctly. You can buy almost anything on credit now a days, which can be good and bad. If you maintain a good credit score and have steady income, you can buy almost anything you want. Let's look at how you can build your credit starting from zero.

If you have no credit history, the best thing to do first is to get a small credit card. Most banks will offer you a balance of $500 or $1,000 for your first card. You can get one from almost any lender, but if you already have a bank account it's easier to get a card through the same bank. This way it will be linked to your current account and it is a lot easier to manage and make payments. If you have online banking, you can transfer the money right out of your account to make a payment on your card. Use your first credit card for small everyday purchases like gas and food. Keep track of how much you rack up and make sure it is something you can pay off within 30 days or else you will be charged interest on the next billing cycle.

Car payments are another great way to build credit. As long as you buy them right and don't overpay. Do your research and only buy what you can afford. Just because you can afford the payments doesn't mean it is a good deal either. If you are paying over 10% interest on a car then you are over paying. Somewhere between 3 and 6% would be ideal depending on what the current rates are. Do the math when they tell you what the payments are and for how long. Multiply the monthly payments by how many months are in the loan and see what the total is compared to the actual price of the car. If you are not sure what you can afford or be approved for, call your bank and ask them. Do not be afraid of the banks, they can be very helpful, and are willing to answer almost any questions you may have. They have a lot of tips and payment calculators too that can help you make a better decision on your purchase. When you are ready to buy a car, do the math and make sure you can afford the payments. Just because you are approved for a certain amount does not mean that you can really afford it. Figure it in with all your other bills and see what will work for you.

Store credit cards can be another way to build credit. They are credit cards that can be used specifically for one store. For example, home improvement stores, furniture stores, electronics stores, and department stores all offer credit cards. They can be a great way to buy big ticket items as well. A lot of stores offer 0% interest financing for 1-2 years on purchases over a certain dollar amount. Need a new tv? Refrigerator? Washer and dryer? New tires on your car? Yes, even tire places offer credit cards with no interest financing. Most people do not have the available cash to purchase these items when they need them, so if you can put them on a store credit card and pay interest free for a year or two, why wouldn't you?

If you have bad credit, it may take some time to repair it. If you have bills that have went to collections, you may want to start there first. There are lots of online sites where you can view your credit report for free. They usually show items that you have in collections too. Call the companies that own your debt and see if they are willing to make a settlement or set up a payment plan. If you are able to, pay off all your items that are in collections. Sometimes you can check the dates on when they will drop off your credit too. After something is in collections for so many years it may have a date of when it is going to drop off your report, meaning it won't show up on your credit report anymore. If something is going to drop off soon, don't worry about paying it off, just wait it out.

The next way to build credit back up is to get a credit card and use it. Make small purchases on a regular basis, and pay them off every month. DO NOT get in the habit of paying the minimum payment on your credit cards! This is how people rack up a lot of credit card debt and cannot get out. Try not to make big purchases that you cannot afford to pay off within a month, unless you are getting a no interest offer. Whenever you make purchases on your credit card, you should keep in mind that you need to pay off the entire balance when your next bill is due so you can avoid paying interest. Make sure you pay them on time too. Making payments on time is a big part of your credit score. If you struggle with remembering when your payments are due, write it down! Make a note on your calendar or write up a bills sheet that has all your bills on it and which days they are due. Post it on the wall of your office, or whichever room in your home that you normally pay your bills.

If you have a lot of credit card debt and cannot seem to get out, there are a few services that can help you out. A lot of credit cards offer 0% interest for the first year. You can transfer your balance to that credit card and pay interest free for one year. Some places offer debt consolidation loans where you can put all your debt on one loan and make one monthly payment. Some loans can be a scam though and may charge a lot of interest. I would avoid most of the offers that you get in the mail. They have a lot of fine print and usually have a high interest rate. Also, you are sending your personal information to a company that you most likely know nothing about. Talk to your local bank or look into some loan offers or credit cards online. Do your research and do the math and see what works best for you.

Credit can be very tricky and easy to mess up if you are not careful. Do not overspend and buy things that you cannot pay off. Take advantage of no interest financing when it comes up. Be responsible and keep track of everything and write it down. Your credit builds the more you use it. Use your credit card, make on time payments, try to avoid high interest, and do not buy things you cannot afford. Do not let credit scare you. If you use it correctly, it can be a very useful tool and a great asset in your financial life.

SECURITY TIPS:

1. **If you are afraid of someone stealing your identity or applying for something in your name, you can freeze your credit.** This prevents anyone from pulling your credit report, even you. If someone were to go to a financial institution and try to open a loan or credit card in your name, they would be instantly denied because the bank or lender would not even be able to pull your credit. It's easy and free to freeze your credit. Just go online to each credit bureau; Transunion, Equifax, and Experian, and find the tab for freezing your credit. This will be permanent until you remove it. Each time you want to apply for a new card or loan you must unfreeze it. There is a way to temporarily lift the freeze and set specific dates for when you want your credit to be unlocked. If you do not want to pay for a credit monitoring service then this is the way to go. By the way, a credit monitoring service cannot prevent all fraud, but it will detect it and notify you when something does happen. People can still open accounts in your name if your credit is not frozen.

2. **Use a credit card over a debit card any chance you get, especially online.** If your debit card number is compromised, then someone may have access to your bank account and all of your money. It can

be a long painful process to get your money back that was taken. If your credit card number however is compromised, they can make charges to your account, but it is easier to dispute. You can cancel your credit card and they will send out a new one. Your bank account has not been compromised and you still have your money. They will dispute the fraudulent charges made on your credit card and take them off.

3. **Be aware of scammers!** I know we all hear this all the time but it is getting worse, and scammers are getting smarter. Unless your job or career requires you to, do not answer your phone if you do not know who it is. If it is important, they will leave you a message and you can call them back. Be careful giving out personal information over the phone. Usually if it is a phone call that you have made to your bank, or some other company you are familiar with, it is ok. But if someone calls you saying they are so and so from a bank or wherever and they are asking for your personal information or saying that you owe them money it is probably a scam. Do not give them any information and just hang up the phone. The same goes for emails too. Companies will not email you at random and ask for personal information. You have to be smart so that your personal information is not compromised. If something doesn't seem right, it probably isn't. Just trust your instincts and think twice before you give someone your information.

4. **Email safety:** Almost everything you sign up for now a days requires you to give them your email address. It can be easy to lose important emails through all of the spam or adds that you may get.

It is a good idea to have 2 or 3 separate email addresses. You can have one that you give out to stores that you shop at or other places that are not super important. You can have another one for your bank accounts or other important accounts. If you are self-employed or own your own business, you should have a separate one for your business too. It is safer to keep your personal, more secure emails in a different account. That way your important email address is not given out to hundreds of people or companies. Remember the more companies that have your information, the easier it is to get lost or stolen.

6. HOW TO MAINTAIN A GOOD CREDIT SCORE DURING HARD TIMES

You may think this title sounds ridiculous and that there's no way to keep your credit up when times are hard. But there is. The main way to keep your credit score up is to use it! Use your credit cards and pay on them over and over again. Often when people come into hardship the last thing they will pay is their credit cards. Well this isn't really the best idea. Sure, you have more important bills like your mortgage/rent and your car payment, but your credit cards are important too. If you fall on hard times and you let your credit score go down, you will be on even harder times. You will not be able to get a loan when you need it or apply for a new credit card, and you will get higher interest rates on any loans that you are approved for. With good credit, you will always be able to loan more money and you will always have a way out.

For example, if you have an unexpected expense and you do not have the money to pay for it, you can put it on a credit card or get a personal loan. The better your credit is, the more opportunities you will have to loan more money. Now you make think you do not want to go into more debt if you are already struggling, but if it's a way out then it's a way out. If you need repairs on your car and you rely on your car to get back and forth to work, then you can use a credit card to pay for those repairs. It may not be the ideal thing to do but at least it keeps you going and you can still get to work. If you have an emergency repair on your home, you can put it on a credit card. If you run out of money for the week, and you need gas in your car, you can use a credit card. Credit can offer you a lot of ways out when the unexpected comes, you just have to be smart about it.

If you find yourself in too much debt, do not panic, get smart. Having a sheet with all your debt laid out (like explained in the previous chapters), will help you out tremendously. You can keep track of each credit card or loan, when it is due, and how much each payment is. Sometimes it is easier to manage more debt if you have multiple credit cards (preferably some that have a high limit and still have a significant available balance). If one of your credit cards comes due and you do not have enough money to pay it in full, you can pay it with another credit card. If you are not able to make a payment directly from credit card to credit card, you can do a cash advance or do a balance transfer. If you do a cash advance, you can take that 'cash' to pay off the credit card that you could not afford to pay. If you do a balance transfer it is either online or through the mail and the credit card company will write a check to the other credit card company to pay the bill. You will then have a bill that is due the next month on a different credit card, but at least you will not be charged interest, and your card was paid on time. That's a win-win in the eyes of the credit bureau and your score will stay up. It's like the old saying 'robbing Peter to pay Paul'. That's essentially what you are doing is transferring your debt to another card to buy you some time and avoid racking up interest.

You can do this as long as you want to, keep chasing credit cards with credit cards to keep them paid until you can afford to fully pay them off. You should pay what you can afford to pay and then transfer or cash advance the rest. This isn't the best habit to get into and you shouldn't rely on it all the time, but it is an option if you can't afford to pay off your cards but you want to maintain a good credit score. You make think this sounds silly because you still have the same debt, but it keeps your credit in good standing. On time payments, high available credit, and low percentage usage on your cards is what will keep your credit up. Use it, use it, use it. Do not stop using credit if you want to maintain a good score. It is possible to be in too much debt and still have excellent credit. It's not always easy and it takes a lot of management and responsibility, but it can be done.

Another way to keep your credit cards paid when you cannot afford to pay them is to put your whole paycheck on your credit card and then use your credit card for bills and expenses. For example, if you owe $375 on your credit card and your paycheck is $400, use your whole paycheck to pay off your credit card! This will keep you from incurring interest which will result in you owing more money. You can then use that same credit card to pay your bills or buy groceries or whatever else you need for the week. Again, you will have the same debt, but you will not be racking up interest and it keeps your credit in good standing. Just like anything else, you have to learn the tricks of the trade to be good at something. There are a lot of tricks and tips to keeping a good credit score, and it can be done whether times are good or bad.

7. HOW TO MANAGE A SAVINGS ACCOUNT

Do you have an emergency fund in savings? You've heard the old saying where everyone should have at least $1,000 in savings at all times. A lot of people do not, and a lot of people think they cannot get there. Well, I'm here to tell you that you can, no matter what your income is. It is not that difficult to put back a little money here and there; you just have to want it and discipline yourself.

If you put back $20 a week every week and did not touch it, after 50 weeks (2 weeks short of a year) you would have $1,000. No amount is too small. Start with whatever you can afford and stick to it. If you can afford more over time, then put more in. But you have to keep it separate from your spending money. Put it in your savings account and DO NOT touch it. If you do not have a savings account, keep it in cash in a safe place in your home but once again, DO NOT touch it.

Do not stop when you reach $1,000. Keep going, putting in a little bit every week. (You will thank yourself later). When there comes a time when you need that emergency money, use it. That's what it is there for. It's up to you what you define as an emergency. (It should be used for something you need, not something you want). A good habit to start is to keep a record of every time you do take money out of savings and write down what you used it for. Keep it somewhere safe so you can reference it later on and you will be able to look back and see where all of your money went. When you take money out of your savings, build it back up. This should be something you do for the rest of your life and make it a priority. Make it a goal to keep $1,000 or $2,000 in savings at all times, and build it back up after you spend it. This will make your life a lot easier and will keep you from making poor financial choices when you need a little extra cash.

This same concept applies when planning for your goals. Do you want to save up for a car or a house? Do you know how much you need to save to make it happen? Figure out a plan and make it happen! Figure up how much you need to save over a certain period of time, and start putting the money back. Make a commitment out of every paycheck and put the money back. For example, if you wanted to save $3,000 for a down payment on a car, and you want to buy the car in 6 months, you would need to put back $115 every week. Print out a picture of what you want to buy for motivation and hang it somewhere in your home where you will see it every day. Or you can make a list of your financial goals and hang them some-where in your home as well. Stay committed and do not give up on yourself!

8. HOW TO BE SMART WITH YOUR TAX RETURNS

Tax returns are something people look forward to every year. When all else fails, you know you have that big chunk of money coming in in the spring. But what do you do with it? Do you go out and buy something that you normally couldn't afford? Do you save it? Spend it on bills? Buy parts or accessories to trick out your car or truck? You can do whatever you want with it, it's your money. But you should be smart about it.

Do you have any bills that are past due? If so then you should probably pay those first. Do you have credit cards or loans that you are paying interest on? Maybe you should pay those off, or at least pay them down as much as you can. Do you owe someone money? Pay them back! It's never good to borrow money from someone and not pay them back, or take too long to pay them back.

Do you need a repair on your car or your house? You could use your tax returns to fix that. Anytime you get a big chunk of money like your tax returns, you should put it to good use. If you let it go to waste you will be kicking yourself for it later. When you get your money, look at all of your expenses and needs. Pay down your debt, use the money for needed repairs, or put it in savings. The last thing you should be doing is throwing your money away and buying things you don't need. Your tax returns are your one freebie per year to get ahead or fix your finances. Be smart and never let a good opportunity go to waste.

9. TIPS ON OWNING A HOME

Owning a home can be a huge asset in your financial life. Whether it's your first home or your third, there are things you can do to put yourself in good financial standing with your mortgage and your property. If you are buying your first home, make sure you pick a good lender. I prefer to go with someone local who has an office or branch I can visit in person if I need to. I also like to make sure they will not sell my loan and my mortgage will stay with them for the entire length of the loan. A lot of mortgage companies sell your mortgage multiple times and then you have to keep up with who to send your payment to whenever it changes. It is good to get a fixed interest rate too. Variable rates are never a good idea because they can cause your payment to go up if the rates go up. They may try to sell you on the idea that it may go down, but there is a chance it could go up too, and you definitely do not want that. Make sure there are no pre-payment penalties too in case you were to pay your loan off before the 30 years is up.

Most banks will recommend that you pay 20% for a down payment, but you do not have to. That would be ideal, but most people do not have that much, especially if you are a first-time buyer. You can still buy the home with less of a down payment (I think the minimum is 3 or 5%) but you will be asked to pay PMI (private mortgage insurance) every month as an additional fee with your mortgage. The fee is usually less than $100 per month and lasts until you have paid down 20% of your original loan balance. There are ways to get rid of your PMI sooner though. If you pay ahead on your mortgage, you will reach the 20% balance faster. Another way is to refinance your home after you have lived in it for a few years. If you have good payment history and you wish to refinance to a 15-year loan instead of a 30, that will eliminate your PMI as well. Your lender can explain all of this to you when you are in the process of buying.

You can also refinance your mortgage and do a cash out loan if you need to make repairs on your house. The bank will require you to have your home appraised again. Based on the appraisal amount, the bank will allow you to borrow up to 80% of your home's value. For example, if your home appraises at $200,000 and you owe $100,000 the bank will let you borrow up to $160,000. The $100,000 will remain from your current loan and the $60,000 would be your cash out money. Your new loan amount would be $160,000 and you would get $60,000 in 'cash' in your bank account to use for home repairs. This is a good option if you need to make expensive repairs on your home and you have positive equity in your property. Negative equity would mean that you owe more on your house than what it is worth.

Always make sure you make your house payments on time. Your mortgage is the most important bill you will ever pay, so make sure it gets paid above everything else. If you are able to pay more every month, then you should. For example, if your payment is $948, try to pay $1,000 or even $1,100. Every little bit counts when you are paying your mortgage. All the extra money will go towards the principal balance and you can pay your home off faster. Another way to get ahead is to make your payment every 4 weeks instead of once a month. There are 52 weeks in a year and if you pay every 4 weeks you will end up making 13 payments in one year instead of 12 if you were to pay it once a month. It's always better to be ahead to give yourself a cushion for a rainy day. If you run into financial trouble and you are a month or 2 ahead on your mortgage, you can skip a payment or pay it 'late' and it will not count against you.

Always keep your house in good working order and presentable to put on the market. If you can help it, try to avoid letting your home become damaged or dirty to the point of where it is unattractive to potential buyers. Your home is an investment and you should always keep resale in mind while you are living in it. You never know what the future will hold or when you may have to sell your house. The last thing you want is to decide you have to sell, and your home is in disarray and you cannot afford to fix it. If expensive repairs arise on your home, like a roof or HVAC system and you can't afford to fix it, look into financing it. Most companies offer financing now a days for big ticket items on your home. If you need a new roof or new HVAC system, most companies will offer financing options for 1 to 3 years. Some of the shorter terms will be interest free, but if you wish to drag it out longer to have smaller monthly payments they will charge you interest, usually somewhere between 8 and 12%. Bottom line is, take care of your home and it will take care of you. The same concept applies to your vehicle too. Try to take care of your vehicle and not trash it and you can get more money out of it when it comes time to sell it.

10. BUYING VS. RENTING A HOME

There has always been a lifelong debate of whether it is better to buy or rent a home. The truth is there is no wrong answer! It's all about your lifestyle and what you prefer. Let's compare the two.

When you own your own home, you must make a big down payment to buy the house and then you have a mortgage with property taxes and insurance for the next 15 or 30 years. (You will still have taxes and insurance after the mortgage is paid off too). You will be responsible for any repairs on the home, no matter how big or small. You will also be responsible for mowing the grass and landscaping too; although you could pay someone to do that if you prefer. On the plus side, you can make any changes to the home that you like. If you want to paint, remodel, hang pictures, change light fixtures, whatever you want to do is totally up to you. This is probably the biggest perk of owning a home is that you can truly make it yours. And since you own it, there will be no fear of being asked to move out if there is a change in ownership of the property; like there could be with a rental. And you will not have to worry about your rent going up like you would if you were renting.

When you are renting your home, the only down payment is a deposit of whatever the rent amount is, plus 1st month rent. You will sign a lease for 6 months or a year and you are locked in for that amount of time. There is no property tax and you are not always required to have renters' insurance, although it is highly recommended that you do. One downside is that you will always have to pay rent the whole time you live there; not like a house where you could potentially pay it off and not have a payment. You are not responsible for any repairs. All of that is taken care of by the owners of the property, or the maintenance crew. Most places will not require you to mow grass, although if you rent a single-family house, you may be asked to. Every private rental is different. On the down side you cannot paint or make changes to the property. The most you can do is decorate with furniture or maybe hang a few small pictures on the wall.

It all comes down to personal preference when it comes to renting or owning. And in some cities, it is too expensive to own so your only option may be to rent. Not all parts of the country are the same when it comes to the cost of housing. If you do not want the headache or responsibility of owning a home, then it is probably better for you to rent. If you prefer your own space and want a house that you can make your own, then it is better for you to own. Just keep in mind you may have to get your hands dirty every once in a while when things need to be fixed.

11. GET YOUR PARTNER ON BOARD

Do you have a spouse or significant other that you live with? Get them on board with your financial goals. Even if you still have separate bank accounts, you still need to be on the same page financially to get ahead. Do not keep any secrets from each other either, it will only hurt both of you in the end.

Talk about everything together. Your bills, savings, extra expenses, goals, everything that involves money. Maybe one or both of you could use some help with your credit. Maybe you have a bad spending habit that you need to quit. Help each other out and make goals together.

Maybe you want to buy a house or take a trip together. Talk it out. Figure out a plan and make it happen. It's easier to do it together and it can be fun too. Hold each other accountable and build each other up throughout the process. After all you are 'partners.' Plan your finances together and you will be amazed at what you can accomplish. The sky is the limit!

12. CLOSING

I hope this book helps you as much as it has helped me. I have really enjoyed writing it. I have always enjoyed working with numbers and money. Everything I know I have learned through my own personal experience. I have also had some good advice from family and fellow coworkers over the years. Make sure to listen to people who are older than you when they are trying to teach you about life. They have been around longer than you, and odds are they have learned a thing or two in their years before you. Another good life tip is to surround yourself with people who are more successful than you and learn from them. Look at some of the things they have done to get where they are. You are never too old or too successful to stop learning or growing as a person. You should always be trying to better yourself throughout your whole life; not just financially but as a person. There is always room for improvement. You should never settle, or think 'this is good enough, I do not have to try anymore.' Your goal should not be to get rich or have a bunch of expensive things you do not need; but to live a more comfortable, stress-free lifestyle. I hope this book can help people to stop stressing about money and to start living again. I have always enjoyed helping people and I hope this book will do just that.

About the Author

I was born in 1991 and was born and raised in Miamisburg, Ohio. I enjoyed color guard and marching band when I was in school. I had a passion for music and really enjoyed playing the piano, but I had no careers in mind with music that would make me any money. I graduated in 2009 with no real intentions of going to college or knowing what I wanted to do with my life. At the age of 19, I found myself working at a manufacturing facility. I stayed there for 10 years; where I met my husband, got married, and had our first child. I learned a lot along the way and took a lot of advice from some of the older guys I worked with. I made decent money working there, so I was able to buy multiple cars, my first house, and opened various credit accounts and loans over the years. Everything

I learned about money and credit I learned through my own personal experience. I became really good at managing our money and credit; and I thought I had learned enough to be able to help people. So, I decided to write this book. Almost 2 years in the making, and I am finally able to present this product to the public. I am a soon to be mother of 2 and a proud wife to my husband of almost 8 years. I owe so much of my success to my husband, but mostly God, who has guided me and kept me safe through the years. My husband has been a great support system to me and we have helped each other grow financially over the years. Neither one of us would be where we are today if it weren't for the other. I am so proud and excited to put this book on the market and I truly hope it changes people's lives. We all have a purpose on this earth and we are all meant to help each other in one way or another. I hope that you find your purpose in life and can find yourself on the path that you were meant to be on!

For more information about any of the budgeting tips and advice in this book, feel free to email the author at YourBestFinancialLife@proton.me.

www.ingramcontent.com/pod-product-compliance
Lightning Source LLC
Chambersburg PA
CBHW070919210326
41521CB00010B/2250